BETWEEN THE DOORS

BETWEEN THE DOORS

Janne —
It is good to be in
community with you.
Many blessings...

Susan Windle

Susan Windle

To order additional copies of this book, contact:
Xlibris Corporation
1-888-795-4274
www.Xlibris.com
Orders@Xlibris.com
21030

Acknowledgements

I am indebted to the teachings of Neil Douglas Klotz for the spiritual and linguistic groundwork of many of these poems. Thanks as always to Wendy for hanging with me for so long, to Annie and Ellen for continual creative conversation, to Pat for many lunches and for reading most of these in raw form, to Sara Steele, Alana Lea, and Constance Wain for visual art that inspires and complements, to the prayer-warriors, war-resisters and peacemakers who give me hope, and to the people of the Unitarian Universalist Church of the Restoration for inclining their ears to my voice.

Contents

To the makers of peace

I want strong peace, and delight,
the wild good.

Muriel Rukeyser

between the doors

all things are possible
i don't mean my house or yours
i don't mean inside or out
that space between
is where i'll meet you

let's stop this back and forth
let's stay right here
in the doorway
where all wars cease

it may seem like a narrow place
where nothing much
could happen
but we can not know the size
of openings we do not see
nor feel the breadth of
that which waits for us

the other side of what seems
impossible

Advent

If I were to write you a December poem
if I were to take the time
from celebrations and preparations for celebrations
from the frantic scurry to the end of the year
the endless wrapping up of business and the fear
that what I have to give
will never be good enough
or that I will give so much
there will be nothing left of me
but a stick and a stone,
if I were to write you a December poem
it would start that small,
that narrow and hard.

But there would be space around it—
a royal sky
around this sliver of moon.
There would be room
for the cold and the bone of it.

And there would be breath.

Into that space
and into that breath
something

would surely drop.

Magnificat

When I opened the doors of my chest
I found your flames inside.
Imagine my surprise—
in the mirror, your face!

On the way to find myself
I met you instead.
In the search for God:
a human being.
In the search for you—
only God.

I do not know what I am—
God, human, you, me.
I know as little and as much
about yourself
(though I see your face
more clearly than my own).

From this confusion
my life is born
again and again and again.

My Faith

Forgive me if my terror shows.
Forgive me, if it doesn't.

Inside is a fear
so great and nameless
I can barely stand here
at your door.

If you find me on my knees,
please understand.
There is something I need
from the stone at your feet.

If I quake but do not bend,
help me down.
There is ground
I know will hold

this wavering soul.

Where School Began

Our dead end street in Paterson was
a carnival of children—
sidewalk chalk and ring-o-leevio,
myself usually among them
on skates or bright red bike.

Six years old, early Saturday morning,
always the first to emerge.
I stretched myself on the back porch step
to face the sky I loved.
Heard my name then
formed in the blue
mouths of clouds
as they rolled and I
with them rolled
in the same wind—
as when I spun like a log
tumbling sky and grass
down the long green hill
on Garrett Mountain.

This also in Paterson,
that gritty town where school began
in the mammoth, macadam playground
and nobody
knew my name.

God, in Paterson

The boy who taught me to ride a bike—
his name was Ron.
At fifteen, he was more than boy.
When he came down to us
from the second story flat
where he lived alone with his mom,
I thought he was a god.
We were all too small
for him to play with,
but still he came
not to tower over us
but to teach—he was so kind.
He took my chalk
and drew a snaky yellow path for me
on that dead end street.
Don't look at your wheels, he said
look at the road I made.

I am sure this was only one
of his many miracles.

Cornmother

Mildred Dunlap Windle (1898-1985)

We husk corn in her backyard:
each lucent, each fragrant ear
whispers *The sun*
comes to the earth.
We touch our cheeks
to its cool kernels,
anticipate
the taste of light.

She is in the kitchen
making salad
for us
deep red tomatoes
thickly sliced.
We offer her our small
pyramid of corn.
She places each ear
into rolling water,
tosses the salad in a silver bowl,
then leaning her large frame
against the kitchen counter,
waits
for the smell of cooked corn
to rise
from the steaming kettle.

She removes each ear,
wraps them together
in white linen,
takes off her stained apron,
sets the platter on the table—
and seats herself
among us.

Whenever we eat
we do this
in remembrance of her.

Lines for a New Friend

for GV

Your friendship
insists sweetly:

you grab the how
steal time from the impossible morning

and set me talking at your kitchen table.

Your nut brown eyes,
the way you carve that peach

remind me of daylight

with breakfast.

Your Drawings

for SS

I love the dangling
pouches of bleedingheart
and the oblique peek
at the graceful
jack-in-the-pulpit.
The decapitated tulip stem
off to the right
of your flared and flaring ones
makes me think
how quickly the month moves
and how tenderly the eye
can hold it.
Then I think of the pencil
in your astonishing hand—

and want to make a frame
for that flower.

Consider the Grass

She doesn't worry
what she produces,
how narrow her life,
what she has to show for it.
She has been growing tall
in the same nook of the river
for years,
suffering all who come here
in their small boats
yearning to be green
and supple like her.
She is married to the sun,
the river bottom, and
the delicious wind.

Even on the stillest of days
she doesn't worry
whether the breeze
will breathe on her again—
has the river stopped?
will the thousand
faces of her self
fall—never to rise again
never to feel

the brush of wings
or watch an iris bloom?
She doesn't worry—
she lives on light.

That's why she stands here
generous and strong.

Morning Glory Seedlings

for AL

I like to think of them growing their
delicate beings in your
moist soil.

I like to think of what can happen
across a continent
with nothing but a prayer
and your hands at work,
training stems I cannot see
on a frame that is not mine
until, until
the insistent tendrils
of that certain vine
find their way up
and up
into the morning
when the first blue wakes you

and blossom after blossom
turns to greet you
every day.

The Visit

for s

Here you are, first time in my garden,
choosing the chair by the fullest roses.

Seeing you this way, your obsidian hair
framed in pink blossoms, my usual life

spins star-ward, to a place I can not name
as you continue speaking in my flowers.

Don't get me wrong—I hear every word.
Your voice, in the luminous evening, is naked and clear.

You talk of ordinary and difficult things:
an old cat, your aging eyes, a close friend

careening into an awful death. There is a light
that pierces through your spoken thoughts,

the same light that pulses through my garden
and shows up in the petals of the Eden Rose

all around your hair.

Garden Gate Café

In memoriam: Elynore Jane Windle (1926-1999)
and the victims of the Kosovo War.

The dangling petals of the weeping cherry
follow me everywhere this spring:
their long pink chains
make a curtain here
for the empty courtyard
a veil
for the stone wall.
They hang so near my face
I feel their softness
through the window pane
and in the sweater
I pull around me, the one
my mother used to wear.
They sweeten everything about this grief,
and fill my eyes
with what I can not speak.

Cluster-bombs. Massacres.
Open pits. Hollow graves.

They whisper *someone weeps*
by every one.
In the upper frame
a willow pours
such tender green,
and grief upon grief is met
with countless blossoms
and the smallest leaves.

April, 1999

2 tsp. lemon rind

Have you ever held a lemon entirely
stripped of its zest?
Have you ever been given
so pale a gift?
Something so tender
it frightens you,
like a bird
fallen from the nest
before its wings—
suddenly there it is in your path
and what are you
to do with it?
or the transparent skin
of your mother
in the hospital bed?
You have been told not to touch
but you must touch
because touch is the only thing
required of you:
the palm of your hand.
The naked, almost skinless fruit
fills it perfectly and jiggles
with juice.
You think of a painting you love:

six bright lemons set in royal blue—
something your eye adores—
but this, this
is sculpture for the blind,
and it has been given
to you.

After The Sound of Tearing Metal

I want to listen only
to the wedge of avocado
protruding softly
from the tough, black hull.
I have already finished eating
but who could resist,
who would even want to,
the whispered invitation
from so smooth a green?

I want to tell how the small chunk
rests on my tongue
and understands everything
I am going to say.
There is no need to chew
a perfect avocado,
nothing effortful or hard,
only the verdant meeting—
flesh on flesh—
and the long, if you let it,

melting away.

Careful

How do you hold a shard of glass?

Not closely,
not in the palm of your hand.
Your skin isn't meant
for the cradling of sharp things.
Pain and blood will tell you:
do not seek warmth
where only the cold shines!
The arctic glaze, however lovely,
will cut to the bone.
Inhabit your fur
when you travel in unforgiving country.
Bring fire from whatever source.
Worship wisely.
At home in your body,
secure in your breath,
adore the beauty
born in the broken glass.

Bow before every bend of light.

Human

Do not be frightened when beauty strikes
though it leaves you mute and sleepless
churning and roiling like a sea
struck by a sudden turn of wind.
It is only the sun that does this—
the source of light plays
through the atmosphere and changes
everything it touches, always.

If this is happening to you in a violent way
threatening your very core
if beauty feels more blade than blessing
your life more blood than stone
be glad in your grief you are human
grateful for the liquid in your pith—lean
into the beauty that never leaves you
the only life that truly lights you.

Arms of the Sea

It happens sometimes.

Nights you cannot sleep.
a prayer you thought you knew
begins to pray you—
words
speak you into being
with a cry, a gasp—
you are gulping for air.

And a breath then
breathes you.

You begin to move
with the tide
of the ocean you are
unafraid of rock,
searching every fissure,
rushing
all the narrow places

with the furthest reaches of your love.

Confession

I have not wanted to be
the sister I am,
sister of the once quick child,
sister of a disordered mind
endless cigarettes and repetitive
cups of tea from the flowered
china cups our mother
once loved.

When I visit the sister I am
I never want to stay.
In the stuffed apartment
smoke crowds my throat.
Pillows of every size piled high
on couch and chair
leave no room
for sitting down,
and mostly
there is nothing to say.

And there is only the same thing
to be heard, over and over,
on any given day.
Today the one thing
is about the white doves
in their cages
how they coo
to the one who cares for them

when the one who cares
is relaxed at home
with her tea.

Today I choose
the chair that leans back perpetually
in the far corner of her room.
The drapes here are always closed.
What lamps there are
she keeps
permanently low.
There is no difference
between night and day here
and that
is the terrible hole
I fear.

Parable of the Lost Coin

for PS

I.

The Coin

Behind a bushel now
in the furthest corner
of an unlit room,
I remember
the moisture of her palm,
the sweet jingle as I dropped
to the others
in her apron pocket.
Ten of us!
in the rhythm of her thighs—
how rich we were then
ready to be changed
to wine, wheat, wood—
anything she needed
for the ones she loves.

II.

The Broom

The freedom of broom
to be nothing but broom,
content
to lean quietly
in the closet
until
at some unforeseen moment
you are gripped from darkness.
With a vigor not your own
by lamps you did not light
you are searching, searching
for something lost,
something dreadfully
needed.

The freedom of broom
to be nothing but broom:
bristle and stick
fierce like wind—
to kiss the stone
to brush the dust away
to reach
into every dark corner
for the missing coin.

III.

The Woman

It's only a drachma, you say.
But that's a day's wage.
What's mine is mine—
every coin is counted.
I do not sleep
when something's wrong
          inside my house.
Call it foolish, this
three a.m. sweeping, but
I am
a lighter of lamps
in the darkest hour.

IV.

The Guests

A party at dawn?
She rouses us from sleep
in the crease of morning
and calls us to her home.
She says she found
what she had lost—
we stumble dimly from our beds.
Look! The sky is apricot—
night leaves grey trails
on her soft face.

She says she knows
how hard our lives have been.
Breakfast all around, she greets—
fish enough for all!
Don't you feel like light yourself,
streaming through her open door?

Morning Glory

There's a star on a vine
by the side of my house—
you can see it untwist
from a bud
tight as a pencil.
If you think the blue
of this unfolding glory
could make you stand
in one place forever,
wait until it opens—
wait until it twirls
inside out.

There's a yellow in the well
of the blue
star's center—
nothing will keep your face
out of that flower.

Another Glory

Just when you think
you've been to the depths
of that blue
a new glory opens
in the shade of a neighboring leaf.
Perhaps because it is
smaller than the others
and darker
beneath its roof of green
you stoop to listen.
What it says is so simple
you dare not say it
but you must somehow
because you have seen it
insist
on the name of the earth
in the heavenly flower.

Turn Back

A child's love is so large
everything you do will be forgiven.
Why do you worry about your crimes
when these wide eyes
want you only to be close?

Father, mother, whoever you are,
painter, poet, whatever your dream,
your sins against the child
need not rule the world.
Stop running now.
Stop the bombing
and the threats of bombs.

Face the one you've hurt.

Peace Poem

The line of this prayer is long, like a seedpod.
We are not alone in this slender case.
Though each attached by a single stalk,
we take our nourishment from the same green wall
as the others who are next to us, very close.
Space is not an issue here—we have enough.
Violence does not enter into it, nor comparisons—
everyone grows. We are each our own
small globe, pleasing to eye, to touch, to tongue
but not so very different from our neighbors,
whose skin is also smooth, whose flesh is sweet.
None of us knows the hour of our fall
or in which way the earth will take us in.
We are here to live the length of our lives
and all we really want to be is food
for those we cannot see.

November, 2002

The News

When you live inside of lies
you burn—
your flame, from a dark cord
deep within you,
lit by a fire
not entirely your own.

You're the candles now
in the misted windows.
Soft and sure and steady
you must stay,
through day and night,
in the one place knowing
you will be seen
by those who seek you

in this obfuscated land.

March 26, 2003

Spring

What say the daffodils
this April morning
as the bunker buster bombs
blast Baghdad
and the show of another war
goes on?

What say the flowers
of the faces,
blistered and blown,
not by an early heat
or a fierce wind
but by devices
sent by men

who should know better
how to care
for blossoming things?

Heavenly Blue

Listen,
this is the blue that sees.

Its clear gaze asks nothing,
wants nothing, misses nothing.

All is forgiven in this flower.

What you cannot accept,
what you outright reject

is taken up in these petals
and turned, held, fed and clothed,

returned to you in a yellow robe

to move like a god
through this world.

Morning Exercises

Early this morning
before my household woke
I heard the sound of the wind
in my hips.
Now, the breakfast dishes cleared,
everyone off to school and work,
I listen again for the *whoosh*.

But hearing only the sound of lists,
I begin to make them,
beginning with the List of Lists
and on to the little lists themselves
the many pressing digits
that shape my daily life.

The wind goes where it lists—
I feel again the swirling
in my sockets
and am brought smiling to myself
or not myself really
but the wind that is me
circling in my bones
and of my bones
and through my bones.

Through the frozen window
winter sun streams from the eastern sky,
the dishwasher sloshes and grunts.
On the oak of my kitchen table
yellow pears ripen on a white plate.
Listen—you can hear them softly
turning, slowly sweetening
with every breath.

The Kiss

for T

There is a kiss—
I know you have received one—
so pure and unmistakable
it leaves you flushed
with a deep, unconditional love.
You can barely believe
your lips—
the moisture
from the petals of this rose
remains on your skin
and you remember
(as you linger
in the freshness of the dawn)
what we poor humans
can do
with our slender lives
when we've been

properly kissed.

This Place

Every so often in the course of seasons
comes a time when you know once again
the place you have chosen to be
is the place that has chosen you.

It's like that now in azalea time
when the face of nearly every stone house
blossoms forth in all manner of pink.
Soft purple and salmon spill

over and down the slopes of yards,
making the very pavement ache.
Cars slow down to listen
to the rolling mezzo
tones of red, and to savor
the smell of earth and sweat
in the thickness of petals.

Every so often comes a time
when you meet the face of your desire
and you choose
to let yourself be wanted.

Ode to Yes

Yes.
Yes is a vulnerable word.
It leaves you wide open
like a tree.

Make the sound.
Notice the longing in the back of your throat.
Send it out now through your lips:
the best dream you have—
full of hope.

It doesn't matter that your leaves
will leave.
It doesn't matter what the others
see or say.
The beautiful yes of trees
will stand

and breathe
life, health
to the struggling creatures
of this world.

Sunflowers

I have seen
the shape
of my soul.

The stem
I struggle to keep straight
is a fluid thing:
the head I would hold up
has no trouble
bowing down.
And what I would keep
new and moist
shrivels
with such ease,
as if my soul enjoys
every second
of its changing form,
and hidden
in each anxious fear is
a long
mellifluous
laugh—

I have met
the shape of my soul.
What cannot be seen
is perfectly
clear.

October Poem

Today I stopped driving and
walked into blue
past the flame gates
of autumn, un-singed
bone-warm.

I have often wondered
what would happen if
I followed the call of my name
every time I heard
colors sing.

Now I am russet, cerulean, October gold.
Once inside the parted
petals of the evening sky
am swallowed
in loamy blackness

into the mouth of
some hungry orchid-
I am that easily
deliciously
changed.

pollinator

heading for the scent
of what i love
i land
on a wetness
that sends me
tumbling
to the bottom
of your cup

though i slip,
though i stumble,
though i bear these heavy,
bewildered wings,
i find in you
a slender door
and narrow myself
through
your needle's eye
the walls of your world,
soft and supple,
push me on
into
that sliver of light—
where day
breaks over me at last

i am coated
in the fragrance of such love
i go
with good news
on my back

Phalaenopsis

Do you think you are
different
from an orchid?
That you've no wings
to spread
from the thickness of you?
or that your throat
should close
before it has fully opened
and called, called to yourself
without tremor
that which you want
and need?
Do you think your fragrance
is anything less than
perfect
or that you won't be seen

for the whole
community of orchids you are
past, present, and future
contained
in one radiant face?

Reflection

These hemlock boughs bending low
over the jade water
will not give up on me,
no matter how long it takes
to understand
the words of this love.
Green to green forever leaning,
the beauty of their form
given back to them
from the liquid depths.

Of course, they do not see this—
they do not need to.
Nor do they know the space between
the river's limpid skin
and the branches' feathered touch
is a holy place, where none
but the breezes enter
and perhaps
the smallest wings.

August

Stay
until you know
when to move—
there's no shame
in being still.
Ask the monarchs in your garden—
they'll tell.

Through the windows
of their wings
at rest
light breaks
through panes of ocher
framed in jet.
The white beads
that dapple the blackness
of their trunks
as they feed
make you wonder
what else
you've not yet seen.

And as you look and look
into the waiting
and the nourishing
at the apex of their arduous lives,
you let go of all thought
that this fluttering life
should change
in any other way
than it is.

Be Perfect

Become ripe,
as the bearer of all fruit
ripens. Be full
and shapely.
Come into your colors
in your own time,
as the source
of all hues
shimmers through you.

Celebrate
the company of others
from different vines.
Enjoy the textures of diverse skins.
Be food with them.
The meal you make together
far surpasses
what you'd be alone.
Fear not the knife
and the mingling

of your oils.

Words So Large

There are words so large
you can live in them.

Isn't it a comfort to know
your fear
is not the biggest thing?

Always, always, if you listen,
a sound will form
around your fragile life.

You can move and breathe
within the dark, expansive
walls of this word.

You can feed
on the juice of its sound.

Outside the Box

Don't try
to fill space
with words.

Let space fill you.

If you speak,
speak only
what the sky

wants.

You will never be wrong.

And think
of all those hues

swirling obediently

from your lips.

Orchid Tells All

However forwardly I face you
however unabashed I am—
these blazing hips, this
open-chested stance—
it's only half the truth.

Look behind me:
see how loosely, how
thinly tethered to the green I am—
continually stepping off my stem
into the cobalt air

where the magenta I meet
mingles with my belly's
yellow fire
and I am charged
with the task of

calling you here.
Color, shape, smell—
every wave of me works
to draw you.
Everything you do in me

will flourish.

Poem-Prints

The following poems from this collection have been integrated into fine art reproductions with the work of painters Alana Lea and Sara Steele:

between the doors, with art by Alana Lea
Consider the Grass, with art by Sara Steele
2 tsp. lemon rind, with art by Sara Steele
Sunflowers, with art by Sara Steele
Outside the Box, with art by Sara Steele
Orchid Tells All, with art by Sara Steele

To view these and other poem-prints please visit *www.susanwindle.com*

About the Cover Art

"Faces of Love" is the poetic name given by the artist to this painting of the Amazon rainforest plant known as mulungu. In Brazil, where this plant grows, it is used to soothe and calm the nerves, and to quiet emotional agitation. "It is simply a flower that spoke to the depths of my heart and asked to be considered, rather than ignored," says the artist. "When Susan presented her poem "Beween the Doors," I felt the two were a perfect match."

Alana Lea is a botanical artist whose work integrates old-world character with contemporary verve. Over the years, she has developed a style that harmonizes beautiful imagery with informative and imaginative wordplays, resulting in spirited showpieces. Her signature works are digital collage featuring exquisitely rendered floral watercolors in a precise, yet lively style. Alana's passion for flowers springs from lifelong awe of the natural world. Nature is a sacred manuscript, she feels, and we can learn every lesson about living by simply observing it closely. A 30-year relationship with the plant kingdom as gardener, herbalist, and entrepreneur, has been food for her soul, as well as a boon to her career as an illustrator.

Alana's watercolors and digital collage giclée prints have been exhibited in the Bruce Museum of Arts and Sciences and the Smithsonian Institute and reside in private collections throughout the United States, Canada and Britain.

A fine art print integrating the cover image and the title poem can be viewed and purchased at www.alanalea.com or www.susanwindle.com.

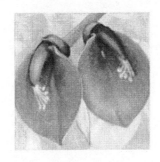

between the doors

all things are possible
i don't mean my house or yours
i don't mean inside or out

that space between
is where i'll meet you

let's stop this back and forth
let's stay right here
in the doorway
where all wars cease

it may seem like a narrow place
where nothing much
could happen
but we can not know the size
of openings we do not see
or feel the breadth of
that which waits for us

the other side of what seems
impossible

BVG